Contents

Friction and resistance experiments and demonstrations

There are several experiments and demonstrations in this book that will help you to understand how friction and resistance work. Each experiment or demonstration contains a list of the equipment you need and step-by-step instructions. You should ask an adult to help with any sharp objects.

Materials you will use

Most of the experiments and demonstrations in this book can be done with objects that can be found in your own home. You will also need a pencil and paper to record your results.

Any words appearing in the text in bold, **like this**, are explained in the glossary.

What are friction and resistance?

Roll a toy car across the floor and it gradually slows down and stops. Walk down a steep hill and your feet do not slide on the pavement. Even if you throw a balloon as hard as you can, it quickly slows down. We see things like this happening every day. They are examples of **friction** and **resistance** at work. Friction and resistance are **forces**.

What are forces?

A force is a push or a pull. Forces make objects start moving, speed up, slow down, stop moving, change direction, or change shape. For example, you push or pull a door to open it. Forces are measured in **newtons** (N). One newton is about the amount of force it would take to lift one apple.

In diagrams we show forces with arrows. The direction of the arrow shows the direction of the force. The length shows the size of the force.

FANTASTIC FORCES

Friction and Resistance

Chris Oxlade

H www.heinemann.co.uk/library
Visit our website to find out more information about Heinemann Library books.

To order:
☎ Phone 44 (0) 1865 888066
📄 Send a fax to 44 (0) 1865 314091
💻 Visit the Heinemann Bookshop at www.heinemann.co.uk/library to browse our catalogue and order online.

First published in Great Britain by Heinemann Library, Halley Court, Jordan Hill, Oxford, OX2 8EJ, part of Harcourt Education.

Heinemann Library is a registered trademark of Harcourt Education Ltd.

© Harcourt Education Ltd 2007

First published in paperback in 2008

Editorial: Nancy Dickmann and Catherine Veitch
Design: Richard Parker and Tinstar Design
        (www.tinstar.co.uk)
Picture Research: Erica Newbery
Production: Vicki Fitzgerald
Index: Indexing Specialists (UK) Ltd

Originated by Modern Age
Printed and bound in China by WKT
  Company Limited

13-digit ISBN: 978 0 431 18041 0 (HB)
11 10 09 08 07
10 9 8 7 6 5 4 3 2 1

13-digit ISBN: 978 0 431 18046 5 (PB)
12 11 10 09 08
10 9 8 7 6 5 4 3 2 1

British Library Cataloguing in Publication Data
Oxlade, Chris
  Friction and resistance. - (Fantastic forces)
  531.1'134
A full catalogue record for this book is available from the British Library.

Acknowledgements
The publishers would like to thank the following for permission to reproduce photographs: Alamy pp. 6 top (Phototake Inc), 6 bot, 9 (Stockfolio), 10 (Buzz Pictures), 16 (The Garden Picture Library), 18 (Anthony Collins), 20 (Joe Fox), 21 (Martin Harvey), 22 (Boating Images Photo Library); Corbis pp. 25 (Peter Johnson), 26 (Reuters/NASA); Getty Images pp. 12, 17 (Photodisc), 23 (Frederic Pacorel/Stock Image); GreatBritishStock.Com p. 13; Harcourt Education Ltd pp. 4, 8, 11, 15, 19, 24 (Tudor Photography); Science Photo Library p. 14 (Philippe Plailly).

Cover photograph reproduced with permission of Getty Images/Mike Powell.

Every effort has been made to contact copyright holders of any material reproduced in this book. Any omissions will be rectified in subsequent printings if notice is given to the publishers.

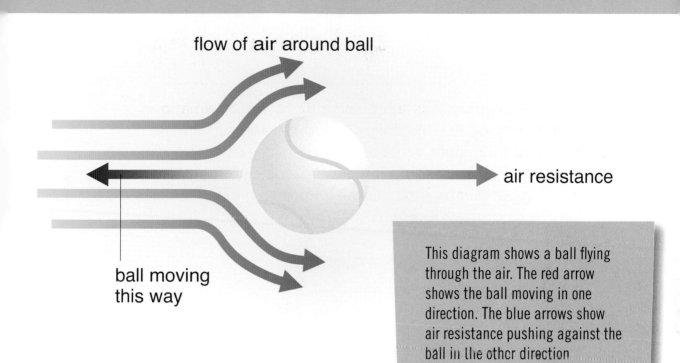

flow of air around ball

air resistance

ball moving
this way

This diagram shows a ball flying through the air. The red arrow shows the ball moving in one direction. The blue arrows show air resistance pushing against the ball in the other direction.

What is friction?

When one thing rubs against another, there is a force between them. The force that you get when two things rub together is called friction. It tries to stop the surfaces sliding past each other. For example, if you try to slide your hand across a table, friction pushes against you. Friction slows down the movement. Friction can stop things moving.

What is resistance?

Air is made up of billions of tiny **particles**. When an object moves through the air, it has to push the particles out of the way to get through. The air pushes back against the object. It causes resistance. The force made by air when it pushes against a moving object is called **air resistance**. Water makes resistance, too. The force that you get when water pushes against an object is called **water resistance**.

What causes friction?

Friction happens because surfaces have tiny bumps and hollows that catch on each other. This makes it hard for one surface to slide across the other. Even surfaces that look very smooth have tiny ridges that you can see through a microscope. A rough surface has bigger bumps and hollows. It normally makes more friction than a smooth surface.

The surface of a wooden floor looks very smooth, but through a microscope you can see the rough fibres that create friction. This photo shows wood seen at 100x magnification.

What materials make high friction?

Some materials make more friction than others. For example, rubber makes a higher friction than plastic. This is because rubber is soft, and the bumps of any material that touches it press into its surface slightly. This makes it even harder for the rubber and the other surface to slide past each other.

Does pressure make friction higher?

Rest your palm flat on a table and try to slide it along. It moves easily. Now press down harder. Is it still easy to push? The friction between your palm and the table gets bigger, the harder you press your hand on the table. When surfaces are pressed together, the bumps and hollows in the surfaces fit together more. It is harder for the surfaces to slide past each other.

DID YOU KNOW?

If there was no friction, life would be very tricky! It would be hard to pick up things with your fingers. Walking would be like walking on ice all the time. Your bicycle tyres would slip on the road.

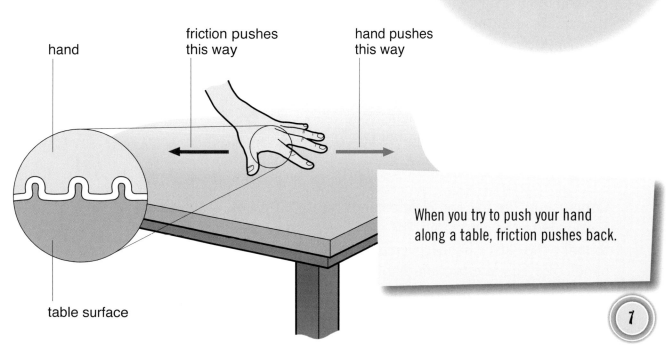

hand

friction pushes this way

hand pushes this way

When you try to push your hand along a table, friction pushes back.

table surface

EXPERIMENT:

Materials and friction

Hypothesis: Rubber bands will create more friction than a box covered in foil.

Equipment: A pile of books, a sheet of card, a long ruler, a small box, kitchen foil, sticky tape, scissors, some elastic bands.

Experiment steps:

1. Cover the small box in foil.
2. Lean the sheet of card against the pile of books to make a ramp.
3. Place the foil box at the top of the ramp. Adjust the height of the pile of books until the box starts to slide down the ramp.
4. Measure the height of the ramp. Make a note of this measurement.
5. Repeat steps 3 and 4 with elastic bands wrapped around the foil box. Try other materials, too.

Conclusion: The foil and elastic bands create different friction with the card ramp. The ramp needs to be steeper to make the elastic band-covered box slide. The elastic bands created more friction than the foil.

Can we reduce friction?

Friction is often a problem. For example, friction between a heavy box and the ground makes it hard to slide the box along. Friction between the moving parts of machines slows the parts down. In cases like this, we try to reduce friction as much as we can. One way of reducing friction is to make a surface as smooth as possible. For example, a playground slide is smooth and polished so that you can slide down as fast as possible. Other things that reduce friction are wheels, machine parts called **bearings**, and liquids called **lubricants**.

What do wheels and rollers do?

It is hard to slide a heavy box across the floor. If you put the box on a trolley, it is much easier to move. This is because the trolley's wheels reduce friction. Instead of the base of the box sliding across the floor, only the smooth wheels go over the floor. There is less friction because a smaller, smooth surface rubs on the floor. Rollers reduce friction, too. If you put some pencil rollers under a heavy brick, it is easier to push the brick along.

Rollers are used in factories to help move things along a production line. These rollers are moving a sheet of metal.

How do bearings work?

Some machines contain metal balls or rollers called bearings. These help reduce friction inside the machine because parts can easily slide over them. Other machines have air bearings that are filled with air. The air stops the parts rubbing together and so reduces friction. There are also machines that have **magnetic** bearings, which use magnets to **repel** each other. This stops parts rubbing together and so reduces friction.

What are lubricants?

A lubricant is a solid, liquid, or **gas** that reduces friction between two surfaces. A lubricant works because it fills the hollows in the surfaces. This stops the ridges catching each other. The most common lubricants are oil and grease.

DID YOU KNOW?

Ice skates let you slide easily across ice. The blades press very hard on the ice and make it melt slightly. This turns the top layer of ice to water. The water works as a lubricant. It reduces the friction between the blades and the ice.

A hovercraft rides on a cushion of air that reduces friction with the water.

DEMONSTRATION:

Reducing friction

This demonstration shows how a hovercraft works.

Equipment: a large balloon, an empty cotton reel, an unwanted compact disc (CD), sticky tape, a sharp pencil, scissors, a balloon pump (optional).

Demonstration steps:

1. Place the cotton reel on the CD so that its middle hole lines up with the hole in the CD. Stick the reel in place with several pieces of sticky tape around its base.
2. Stretch the neck of the balloon over the top of the cotton reel.
3. Inflate the balloon by blowing or pumping air through the cotton reel. Squeeze the neck to stop the air escaping.
4. Place the CD on a smooth table. Release the neck and give a gentle push to set the hovercraft going.

Explanation:

The air rushes out of the balloon. It spreads out under the CD and makes a cushion of air. The cushion of air works as a lubricant. It reduces friction between the CD and the table.

Can we increase friction?

Sometimes we actually increase **friction** on purpose to stop things sliding about accidentally. For example, shoes have a rubbery sole with a pattern of grooves called a **tread**. The tread makes the sole of the shoe bumpy and increases the friction between the shoe and the ground. It stops you slipping when it is wet or muddy. Steps and ramps often have a pattern on them, too, which also increases friction.

Many objects, such as chairs, tables, and lamps, have rubber feet. The soft rubber increases friction between the object and the floor, which stops the object sliding about. Rubber bath mats stop you slipping in the bath, and rubber handles on bats and rackets help you to hold them firmly.

Rock climbers wear special climbing shoes with soft rubber soles. Tiny bumps in the rock surface press into the rubber. This creates very high friction between the rock and rubber that stops the shoes slipping.

Bicycle brakes have rubber blocks that make friction when they press against the wheel rim.

DID YOU KNOW?

Most tyres have a tread. The tread squeezes water away from under the tyre so that it can grip the road. If there was no tread, the water would work as a **lubricant**. The water would make the car skid.

How do tyres work?

Most road vehicles have rubber tyres with a pattern of deep grooves. The tyres increase the friction between the vehicle's wheels and the road. They help the vehicle wheels to grip the road as the vehicle speeds up and brakes. They also stop the wheels skidding on corners. Racing cars have wider tyres. The wider tyres make more friction, as more tyre rubs against the road. This helps the racing car tyres to grip better on the track at very high speeds.

Do brakes use friction?

Brakes slow a vehicle down. The most common type of brake is called a disc brake. It has a metal disc on the wheel and two brake pads. When the driver presses the brake pedal, the brake pads press on each side of the disc. The pads and the disc rub together and make friction. The friction slows down the disc. The disc is attached to the wheel, and so the wheel slows down too.

What causes air resistance?

Air is a **gas** that is all around us. It seems very thin and light, but it is probably heavier than you think. It is made of tiny **particles** called **molecules**. There are billions of them in a thimble-full of air. Your bedroom probably has about 20 kilograms (44 pounds) of air in it! When an object moves through the air it has to push the air molecules in front of it out of the way, and the air has to flow around it. The air pushes back against the moving object. This push is called **air resistance**, or **drag**.

Does speed affect air resistance?

The amount of air resistance on a moving object depends on the object's speed. A fast-moving object has to push more air molecules out of the way more quickly than a slow-moving object. This means that more air molecules push back on the faster-moving object, making more air resistance.

A **wind tunnel** is used to measure the air resistance of objects. Here a skiing helmet is being tested.

Does shape affect air resistance?

Air resistance also depends on the shape and size of an object. Objects with smooth, rounded shapes, such as balls, normally move through the air more easily than objects with flat faces and sharp edges, such as cubes. The air resistance on smooth shapes is less.

EXPERIMENT:

Paper drop

Question: Will crumpled paper reach the ground before a flat piece of paper?

Hypothesis: The crumpled paper will reach the ground first.

Equipment: 2 sheets of paper the same size.

Experiment steps:
1. Crumple one sheet of paper into a ball.
2. Hold the crumpled paper in one hand and the flat sheet in the other hand.
3. Drop the paper from the same height, at the same time.

Conclusion: The crumpled ball of paper falls to the ground first. The flat paper has a greater surface area pushing against the air on its way down. There is less air resistance on the crumpled paper, so it falls more quickly.

What is terminal velocity?

When you drop an object through the air, two **forces** act on it. **Gravity** pulls downwards, and air resistance pushes upwards. At first, gravity is greater than air resistance. This makes the object speed up. It is **accelerating**. But as it falls faster, air resistance increases. Eventually the air resistance pushing up is as great as the gravity pulling down. The two forces cancel each other out. Now the object stops accelerating. It continues down at the same speed. This speed is called **terminal velocity**.

When a drop of rain reaches the ground, it is moving at terminal velocity.

Can we reduce air resistance?

Air resistance is often a problem, especially in transport. Air resistance affects all forms of transport, from motorcycles to jet airliners. A vehicle needs **energy** to push against air resistance. A vehicle burns **fuel** such as petrol to give it energy. Making air resistance as small as possible means vehicles need less energy. This means that vehicles burn less fuel. This saves money. It is also good for the environment because burning fuel creates **pollution**. The faster a machine travels, the more it is affected by air resistance. This means that air resistance is much more of a problem for a fast jet airliner than for a slow bicycle.

Birds are streamlined to help them fly through the air. Their feathers point backwards so air can easily flow over them.

What is streamlining?

A streamlined object is shaped so that air can flow easily around it. This reduces the air resistance as much as possible. Streamlined objects have a smooth shape, and often have a rounded front and a pointed back. For example, an aeroplane has a rounded nose, a smooth body, and a pointed tail.

Why do cars have a top speed?

The faster a car goes, the greater the air resistance it has to push against. The amount of air resistance increases very quickly as the car speeds up. Eventually, the **resistance** gets so high that it cancels out the push from the engine trying to make the car go faster. The car cannot go any faster.

DID YOU KNOW?

After an aeroplane takes off, it climbs to a height of about 10,000 metres (33,000 feet). The aeroplane travels at this height as air resistance is lower here than on the ground. Air resistance is lower because there are fewer air **molecules** in the air. There is less air to push out of the way. The jet can travel faster.

Even cyclists have a top speed. Air resistance will eventually cancel out the push from their legs.

EXPERIMENT:

Testing shapes

Question: Which shapes make most air resistance?

Hypothesis: Shapes with flat faces and edges will make more air resistance than rounded, smooth shapes.

Equipment: 4 pieces of card, sticky tape, scissors, a hairdryer.

Experiment steps:
1. Roll one piece of thin card into a round tube.
   Tape it up to stop it unrolling.
2. Fold another piece of card into a square tube. Tape the edges together.
3. Tape up the third piece of card to make a fish-shaped tube.
4. Stick each tube on to a card base. Put them side-by-side on a table.
5. Blow air at them with a hairdryer from about 1 metre (3 feet) away.
   Gradually move the dryer closer.

Conclusion: The square-shaped object moves first, and the fish-shaped object moves last. This shows that shapes with flat faces and edges make more air resistance than rounded, smooth shapes.

Can we increase air resistance?

Sometimes we want to increase **air resistance**. We normally do this to help slow down objects that are moving along or falling at high speed.

How does a parachute work?

A parachute creates air resistance to slow down a falling skydiver or supplies dropped from a cargo aircraft. Parachutes trap air **molecules** underneath them. The trapped air molecules push up against the parachute and slow it down. Spacecraft designed to return to Earth or land on other planets or moons have parachutes that slow them down after they have entered the **atmosphere**.

Birds use air resistance to help them slow down. They spread out their wings to increase the amount of air resistance.

DID YOU KNOW?

Air resistance is the **force** that makes your hair fly back as you ride along on a bicycle. It also makes your hair fly back when you stand facing into a strong wind. This is because standing still in the wind makes air flow around you in exactly the same way as moving through the air.

This airliner has lowered its wing flaps. The flaps increase air resistance, which slows the aircraft as it approaches the runway.

Can air slow vehicles down?

Air resistance is used to slow some vehicles travelling at high speed. Drag-racing cars have parachutes that help to slow them down at the end of a race. Aircraft have air brakes. These are flaps that extend down from the wing. The flaps push against the air and increase the air resistance. Racing motorcyclists crouch down on straight parts of the track. Less of their body pushes against the air. This reduces air resistance. They lift their heads before corners to increase air resistance and help with braking.

Do liquids make resistance?

Like air, liquids are made up of billions of tiny **particles**. When an object moves through liquid it has to push the particles out of the way to get through. The liquid pushes back against the object. It causes **resistance**. For example, you can feel the resistance of water push against you as you swim in a swimming pool. The particles in liquids are packed together more tightly than the particles in air. They are **denser**. This means they create much more resistance than air.

How does a liquid affect resistance?

The more dense the liquid, the bigger the resistance is. This is because denser liquids have more particles or **matter** for an object to push out of the way. Thick liquids also create more resistance. For example, cooking oil is thicker than water. Cooking oil creates more resistance than water.

A hydrofoil reduces the resistance against it by riding on underwater wings.

SHEARWATER 6

The streamlined shape of this dolphin allows it to swim fast with little effort.

DID YOU KNOW?

The particles of a liquid rub against the surface of a moving object. This rubbing is called **skin friction**. Sharks have very tiny ripples on their skin that some scientists think reduces skin friction by letting water flow very smoothly over the skin.

Can we reduce liquid resistance?

As with **air resistance**, liquid resistance in water is often a problem for transport. Vehicles such as boats have to push against **water resistance**. The water resistance slows them down and they use up lots of **fuel**. Liquids flow around objects with a streamlined shape more easily. Boats, ships, and submarines are built with streamlined shapes to help them move more easily through the water. Water resistance is also a problem for animals that live in the water. This is why most fish have a streamlined shape, with a rounded front and thin tail. This lets them swim **efficiently**.

EXPERIMENT:

Boat race

Question: Do different-shaped boats create different resistance in the water?

Hypothesis: A pointed shape will make less resistance than a flat shape.

Equipment: Card, kitchen foil, cotton thread, a deep tray, scissors, modelling clay, rice, sticky tape.

Experiment steps:

1. Cut out one square of card and one long diamond-shaped piece of card.
2. Tape strips of card to the edges of the square and the diamond to make two boats.
3. Cover the boats in foil to make them waterproof. Half fill them with equal amounts of rice.
4. Fill the tray with water. Place it with one edge just over the end of a table.
5. Cut two pieces of cotton. Tape a piece of cotton to the front of each boat.
6. Put two blobs of modelling clay exactly the same size on the ends of each piece of cotton.
7. Place the boats in the water, with their fronts level. Hang the cotton threads over the edge of the table. Release both boats together.

Conclusion: The diamond-shaped boat moves through the water more quickly than the square-shaped boat. This shows that a pointed shape makes less resistance than a flat shape.

Does friction make heat?

On a cold day you rub your hands together to warm them up. This works because of **friction**. When two surfaces rub against each other, the friction makes heat. The harder the surfaces are pressed together and the faster they move, the more heat they make. Friction between a match and its box creates heat to light the match.

Is heat from friction a problem?

Vehicle brakes use friction to slow down the vehicle. The friction makes heat. This heat makes the brakes hot. The brake parts are made from materials that are not damaged by high temperatures. Normally, they cool down again when they are not being used. However, using brakes for too long without stopping can make the parts so hot that they melt. Racing cars use their brakes so much that they can become red hot. They are cooled by air flowing over them.

DID YOU KNOW?

Rubbing two pieces of wood together is one way to start a fire without matches. The end of a special stick is pressed on to a sheet of wood and spun backwards and forwards very quickly. Friction heats the wood, making red-hot sparks that are used to light the fire. Fire can be dangerous, so do not try this yourself.

Twisting the top stick very fast creates enough heat to make the wood glow red hot.

Does air resistance make heat?

When an object moves through the air the **particles** in the air rub against it. This rubbing is called **skin friction**. When an object moves through the air extremely fast, skin friction makes the object's surface incredibly hot. For example, when a spacecraft re-enters Earth's **atmosphere** from space at high speed, skin friction heats it up so much that it glows red hot.

Heat-resistant tiles protect a space shuttle from the heat made by friction as the shuttle hurtles back into the Earth's atmosphere at the end of a mission.

Can we get rid of friction and resistance?

Friction and resistance happen everywhere on Earth. When they are useful, we make them as large as possible. At other times, we want to reduce them as much as possible. However, no matter how hard we try, we cannot get rid of them completely. The only place where **air resistance** does not exist is in space, where there is no air. This is why spacecraft can turn off their engines when they reach space. They carry on travelling at the same speed because there is nothing to slow them down.

What is perpetual motion?

Friction and air resistance always slow down and stop machines on Earth. The machines cannot keep going unless some power or **energy** is put into them all the time. In the past, many people believed that they could build machines that would keep going forever, once they had been started. These were called perpetual motion machines. However, they all failed.

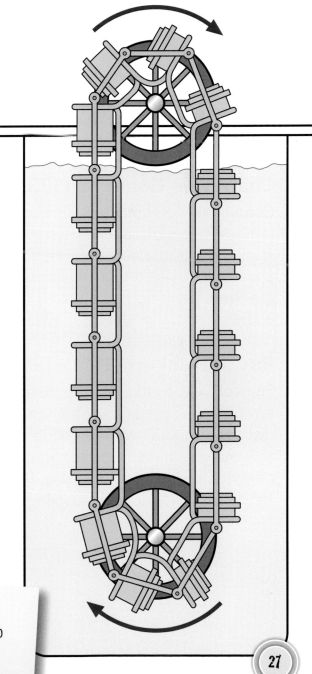

This perpetual motion machine uses air-filled containers that float. But friction and **drag** stop it from working.

People who found the answers

Leonardo da Vinci (1452–1519)

Leonardo da Vinci was a man with many talents. He was a skilled painter (he painted the famous *Mona Lisa*) and sculptor, and also an engineer and scientist. **Friction** was one of the many things he studied. He worked out that heavier objects create more friction, and designed different **bearings** to reduce friction.

Charles de Coulomb (1736–1806)

Charles de Coulomb was a French scientist. He is most famous for his discoveries about electricity, but he also studied friction. He knew nothing about Leonardo's work, and he discovered that the force of friction depends on the **force** pressing two surfaces together. This became known as Coulomb's Law of Friction.

Roy J. Plunkett (1910–1994)

Plunkett was a chemist who discovered a material with very low friction, called polytetrafluoroethylene. He made his discovery in 1939 while working for the DuPont company. This material has the trade name Teflon. It is used in machine bearings and in non-stick pans. Plunkett actually discovered Teflon by accident while working with other chemicals.

Amazing facts

- The wheel was invented about 5,500 years ago. Until then everything was carried by people, animals, sledges, or boats. Huge blocks of stone, such as the ones used to build the pyramids in Egypt, were moved with wooden rollers.

- Small spiders can travel many kilometres through the air. They let out a silk strand, which creates high **air resistance**. This gives the spider a **terminal velocity** so low that a rising air current can lift it up and carry it along.

- Some swimmers wear a special swimming suit with a surface just like the rippled skin of a shark. The suit is supposed to let them swim a tiny bit faster.

- Racing car tyres are very soft so that they make plenty of friction with the track. But they wear away quickly and only last for one race!

- **Magnetic** levitation trains are not slowed by friction. They have powerful magnets that stop them touching the track. A Japanese experimental maglev train has reached 580 kilometres (363 miles) per hour.

- The first person to use a parachute to save his life was Frenchman Jean Pierre Blanchard. He jumped from a damaged hot air balloon in 1793.

- When a space shuttle re-enters Earth's **atmosphere** it is travelling at more than 25,000 kilometres (15,600 miles) per hour. Friction with the air heats the underside of the shuttle to about 1,600°C (2,900°F). Special **ceramic** tiles protect the craft from this intense heat.

Glossary

accelerate increase speed

air resistance pushing force of air molecules against a moving object. Force that slows down objects moving through the air.

atmosphere air surrounding Earth

bearing part of a machine that lets another part spin around easily. Most contain metal balls or rollers.

ceramic material made by heating clay or other material to make it hard

dense tightly packed together

drag another word for air resistance

efficiently working well with little waste

energy stuff that makes things happen. You get energy from food. Electricity is energy, and so are heat, light, and sound.

force push or pull that makes an object move, speed up, change direction, or slow down

friction force caused by contact between the surfaces of two objects. Friction slows down movement.

fuel material, such as petrol, that is burned to give power to a machine

gas substance with widely spaced molecules that can expand to fill the space it is in

gravity force that pulls all objects towards the centre of Earth

lubricant solid, liquid, or gas between two surfaces that reduces the friction between the surfaces

magnetic force between magnets

matter stuff that everything in the universe is made of

molecule tiny amount of a substance

newton unit that measures a force

particle a very small piece of material

pollution anything put into the environment that is harmful to nature

repel push something away

resistance pushing against something

skin friction force created when air or liquid molecules rub against the surface of an object

terminal velocity maximum speed of a falling object

tread pattern of grooves on a tyre or the bottom of a shoe

water resistance force that tries to slow down objects moving through water. It increases with speed.

wind tunnel wide tunnel through which air is blown. Wind tunnels are used to test the air resistance of different objects.

Further information

Books

Can You Feel the Force?, Richard Hammond (Dorling Kindersley, 2006)

Fusion: Roller Coaster!, Paul Mason (Raintree, 2007)

Fusion: The Extreme Zone, Paul Mason (Raintree, 2007)

Science Answers: Forces and Motion, Chris Cooper (Heinemann Library, 2004)

Science Files: Forces and Motion, Chris Oxlade (Hodder Wayland, 2005)

Tabletop Scientist: Air, Steve Parker (Heinemann Library, 2005)

Websites

You can try some interactive experiments on air resistance and friction at *http://www.bbc.co.uk/schools/scienceclips/ages/10_11/forces_action.shtml*

If you want to see if an elephant or a feather will fall faster, visit *http://www.physicsclassroom.com/mmedia/newtlaws/efar.html*

Learn more about the forces that affect parachutes at *http://www.seed.slb.com/en/scictr/watch/skydiving/gravity_drag.htm*

Check out examples of perpetual motion machines at *http://www.lhup.edu/~dsimanek/museum/unwork.htm* – none of them work!

Index